Voices of Animals in Other Lands

By

Kath Mitchell

VOICES OF ANIMALS IN OTHER LANDS

Copyright © 2025 all rights reserved.

Printed in United States of America

Thank you for buying an authorized edition of this book and for complying with copyright laws by not reproducing, scanning, or distributing any part of it in any form without permission.

ISBN: 979-8-9888025-7-0

Publisher: Manhattan Publishing House

Dedication

To all who believe in my gift, support my voice,
and stand by my first Published book, thank you.
Your encouragement means more than a stack of
picture books reaching from the Earth to the Moon.
You give me the confidence to keep growing, creating, and dreaming.
Now, I'm proud to share with you the second edition of
Voices of Animals in Other Lands
with brighter, more beautiful illustrations and a cleaner,
more inviting format for young readers and their grown-ups.
This edition is especially meaningful to me
not only because of what's been improved,
but because it shows how creativity grows, just like we do.
I hope this hardcover copy finds a lasting place in your heart
and on your bookshelf.

With all my gratitude,

Kath Mitchell

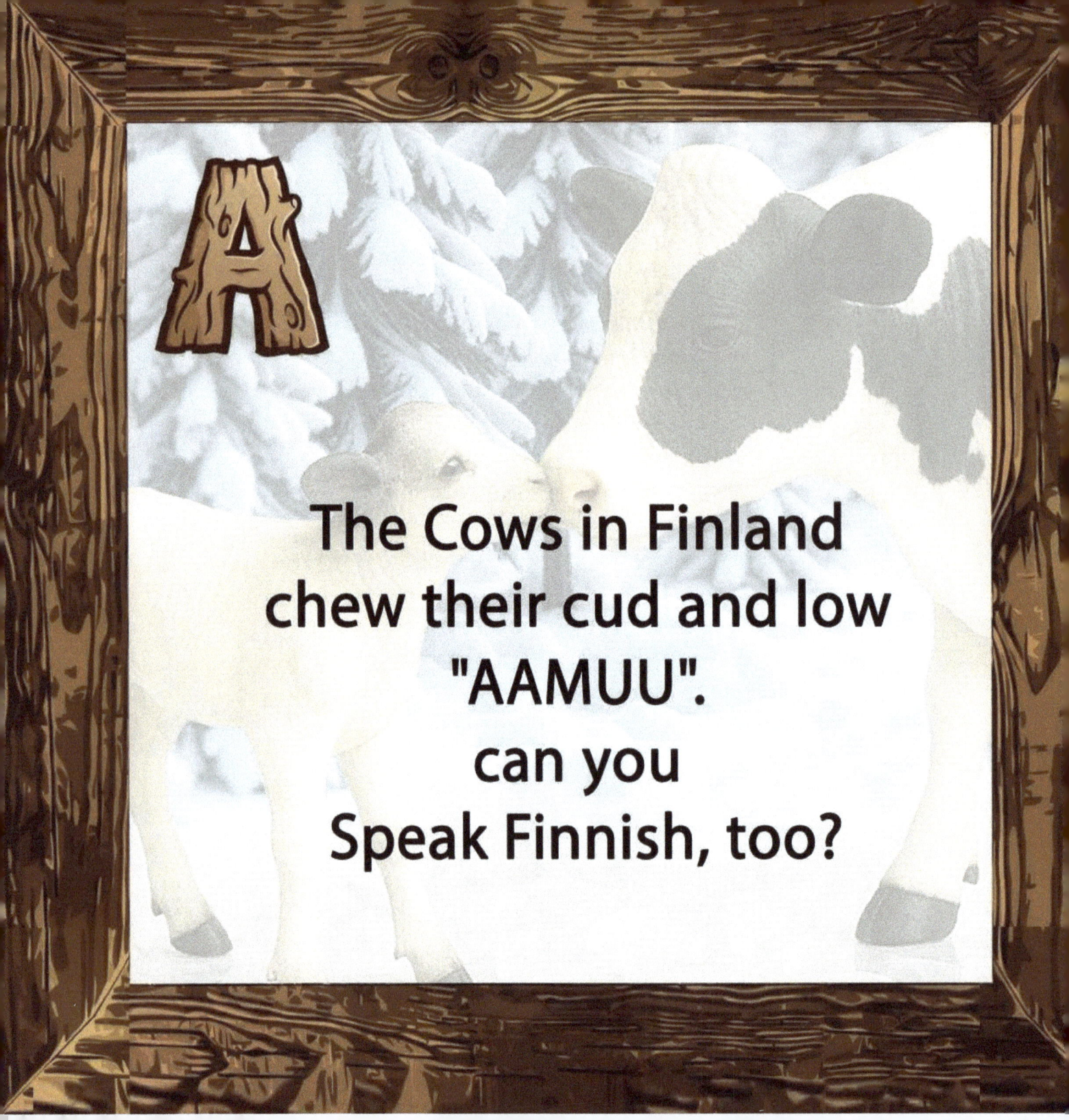

D

Rabbits
World wide are mum.
When they sense danger,
They use their
Back feet to "DRUM"

"EEYORE" is the British Donkey's sound. Where can a Famous English Donkey named "EEYORE" be found?

Donkeys in Poland Bray, "L-A-I-A"

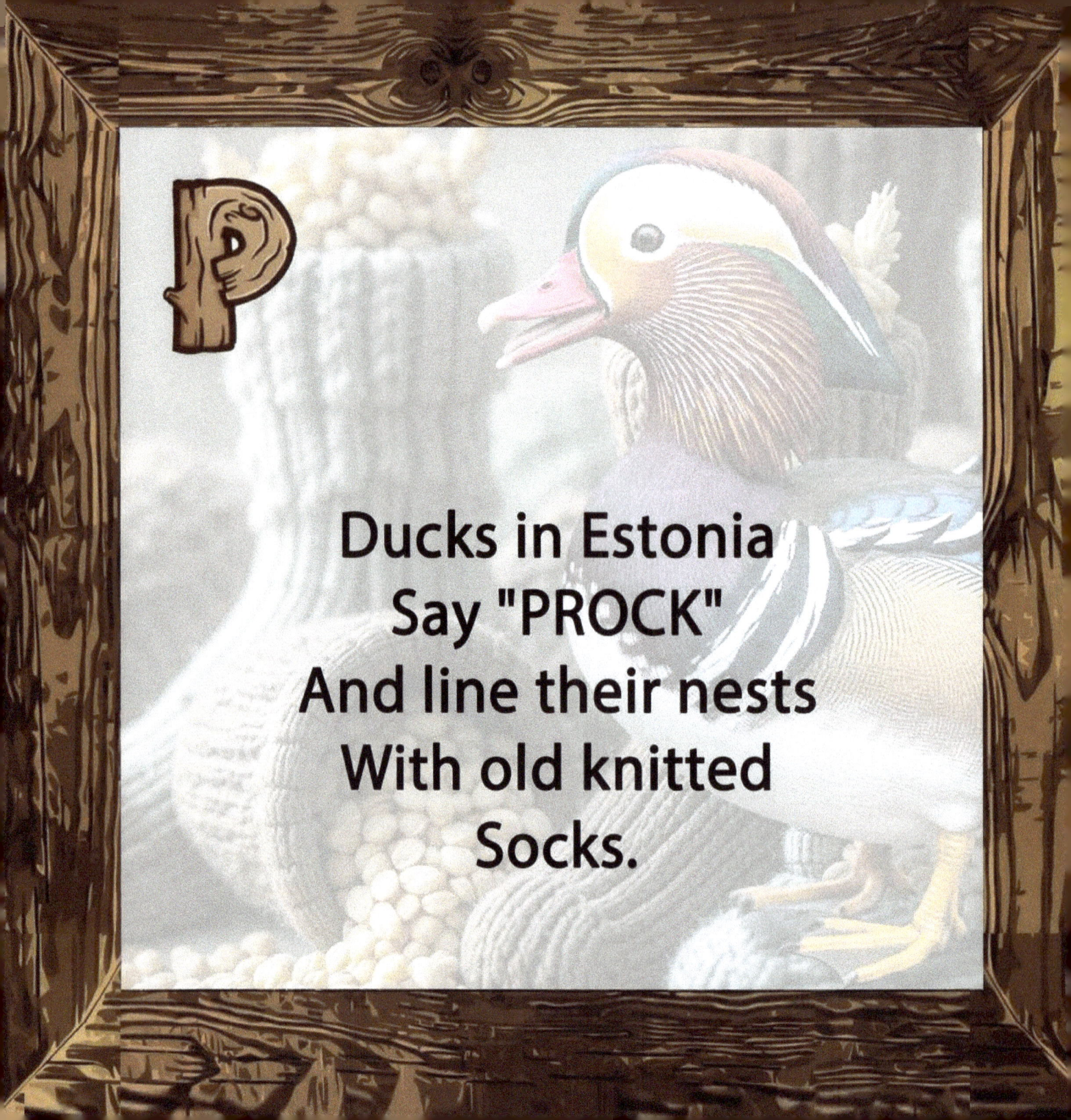

www.ingramcontent.com/pod-product-compliance
Lightning Source LLC
Chambersburg PA
CBHW061942130526
44582CB00042B/94